RHINE RIVER CRUISE

TRAVEL GUIDE

2024/2025

Experience Charming Riverside Towns and Cities

Ann S. Moorehead

Content

3

ENJOY YOUR RHINE RIVER CRUISE!

Introduction

Welcome to Your Ultimate Rhine River Cruise Guide

Ⅰt was a crisp morning in late September when I first set foot on the deck of a Rhine River cruise ship. As I stood there, with the early morning mist gently lifting off the water, I felt a profound sense of anticipation and excitement. I had spent months planning this journey, dreaming of the historic towns, stunning landscapes, and the unique cultural experiences that awaited me along the Rhine. As the ship slowly began its journey, gliding smoothly over the calm waters, I realized that this was not just a vacation; it was an adventure that would forever change my perspective on travel.

Hello, fellow traveler! My name is Ann, and I am thrilled to be your guide on this extraordinary journey along the Rhine River. Over the years, I have had the privilege of exploring many parts of the world, but the Rhine holds a special place in my heart. This river, with its rich history, picturesque villages, and magnificent castles, offers an experience unlike any other. My goal with this guide is to share with you not just the practical information you need, but also the stories, insights, and little-known secrets that make the Rhine so enchanting.

How to Use This Guide

This guide is designed to be your comprehensive companion as you embark on your Rhine River cruise. Whether you're a first-time cruiser or a seasoned traveler, you'll find valuable information to enhance your journey. Here's how to make the most of this guide:

1. Planning Your Trip: Start by reading the chapters on preparing for your journey. These sections cover everything from choosing the right cruise to packing essentials, travel documents, and budgeting tips. This foundational information will ensure you're well-prepared and excited for your adventure.

2. Itineraries and Routes: Once you have the basics covered, dive into the itineraries and route plans. Here, you'll find detailed day-by-day plans and customizable options to suit your preferences. This will help you visualize your journey and make the most of each stop along the way.

3. Destinations and Stopovers: The heart of your cruise will be the destinations you visit. Each chapter dedicated to key destinations provides an in-depth look at what to see and do, from must-visit landmarks to hidden gems. Use these sections to plan your shore excursions and make every stop memorable.

4. Activities and Adventures: Beyond sightseeing, the Rhine offers a wealth of activities. Explore chapters on hiking,

cycling, wine tasting, and more to enrich your experience. These activities will help you connect more deeply with the places you visit and create unforgettable memories.

5. Cuisine and Dining: One of the joys of travel is discovering new foods. Our guide to Rhine Valley cuisine will introduce you to regional specialties and the best places to dine. Don't miss the sections on food festivals and culinary events to savor the local flavors.

6. Practical Tips: Traveling can come with its own set of challenges, so we've included practical travel tips on navigating the Rhine, communication, currency, and staying connected. These tips will help you travel smoothly and confidently.

7. Enhancing Your Experience: To make your trip even more special, we've included chapters on photography tips, journaling, shopping for souvenirs, and making the most of your downtime. These sections will help you capture and cherish every moment of your cruise.

8. Special Interests: Whether you're traveling with family, solo, or looking for a romantic getaway, we've got you covered. Our special interest sections provide tailored advice to ensure every traveler's needs are met.

As you read through this guide, you'll notice a blend of factual information, personal anecdotes, and practical advice. This mix is designed to keep you engaged, informed, and inspired. I encourage you to take notes, highlight sections, and refer back to this guide throughout your journey. It's not just a book; it's your travel companion, filled with insights that will make your Rhine River cruise truly exceptional.

Thank you for choosing this guide. I am honored to share this journey with you, and I can't wait for you to experience the magic of the Rhine. Bon voyage!

Overview of the Rhine River: History and Significance

The Rhine River, one of Europe's most iconic waterways, flows majestically from the Swiss Alps to the North Sea, stretching over 1,230 kilometers (about 765 miles). This river, steeped in history and natural beauty, has been a lifeline for civilizations, a strategic military route, and a source of inspiration for countless artists, poets, and composers.

A Historical Lifeline

The Rhine has served as a crucial artery for trade and transportation since ancient times. The Romans recognized its strategic importance and established numerous settlements along its banks. They built fortresses and roads that facilitated the movement of goods and troops, transforming the Rhine into a bustling trade route.

During the Middle Ages, the Rhine's significance only grew. Its waters linked the North Sea with the interior of Europe, allowing for the exchange of commodities like wine, grain, and textiles. The riverbanks became dotted with castles and fortifications, each vying for control over the lucrative trade passing through. These castles, many of which still stand today, tell tales of feudal rivalries and romantic legends.

Cultural Significance

The Rhine is not just a river; it's a cultural symbol. It has inspired a wealth of mythology, including the legendary

Lorelei rock, where a siren is said to have lured sailors to their doom with her enchanting song. This myth has been immortalized in poetry and music, notably in Heinrich Heine's poem "Die Lorelei" and the operas of Richard Wagner.

The Romantic movement of the 19th century saw a renewed interest in the Rhine. Artists and writers flocked to its shores, capturing its scenic beauty and historic ruins in their works. The river became synonymous with romanticism, evoking images of knights, castles, and picturesque landscapes.

Modern Importance

Today, the Rhine remains a vital commercial route, bustling with cargo ships and tourist cruises. It flows through six countries—Switzerland, Liechtenstein, Austria, Germany, France, and the Netherlands—connecting major industrial regions and vibrant cities. Its banks are home to some of Europe's most important economic centers, including Basel, Strasbourg, and Rotterdam.

The river also plays a crucial role in environmental sustainability. Efforts have been made to clean its waters and protect its ecosystems, making it a haven for wildlife and a source of clean drinking water for millions.

In essence, the Rhine is a river of contrasts—historical yet modern, natural yet industrial, serene yet bustling. As you embark on your cruise, you'll journey through time and space, experiencing the very heart of Europe in all its complexity and beauty.

Planning Your Trip: Best Times to Cruise the Rhine

Choosing the right time for your Rhine River cruise is essential to making the most of your journey. The Rhine's charm varies with the seasons, and understanding the advantages of each can help you plan an unforgettable trip.

Spring (March to May)

Spring is a magical time to cruise the Rhine. As the riverbanks burst into bloom, the landscapes transform into a vibrant tapestry of colors. The vineyards come alive with budding vines, and fields of tulips in the Netherlands create a breathtaking sight. Temperatures are mild, making it perfect for outdoor excursions.

Events to look forward to in spring include the famous Tulip Festival in the Netherlands, where you can witness endless fields of tulips in full bloom. Spring is also the season for various local festivals celebrating the arrival of warmer weather, providing an authentic taste of regional culture.

Summer (June to August)

Summer is the peak season for Rhine River cruises, and for good reason. The weather is warm, the days are long, and the towns along the river are bustling with activity. It's the perfect time to enjoy the Rhine's outdoor attractions, such as hiking, cycling, and wine tasting.

One of the highlights of a summer cruise is the Rhine in Flames festival. This spectacular event features fireworks displays illuminating the castles and riverbanks, creating a magical atmosphere. Summer is also the best time to experience the local cuisine, with many outdoor markets and wine festivals showcasing the region's culinary delights.

Autumn (September to November)

Autumn is perhaps the most picturesque time to cruise the Rhine. The vineyards and forests along the river turn brilliant shades of red, orange, and gold, creating stunning scenery. The weather is still relatively mild, and the summer crowds have thinned out, offering a more relaxed experience.

The autumn harvest season brings a host of wine festivals, where you can sample the new vintages and enjoy traditional food and music. The famous Oktoberfest in Germany is also a short detour from the Rhine, providing an opportunity to experience one of the world's most renowned cultural celebrations.

Winter (December to February)

Winter cruises on the Rhine offer a unique and enchanting experience. The towns and cities along the river are adorned with festive decorations, and the Christmas markets are in full swing. These markets, famous for their handcrafted goods, mulled wine, and holiday treats, are a highlight of any winter cruise.

While it's colder, the winter season provides a cozy and intimate atmosphere. The snow-covered landscapes and twinkling lights create a fairy-tale setting. It's also the best time to visit the grand cathedrals and historic sites without the summer crowds.

Practical Considerations

- Weather and Clothing: Pack appropriately for the season. Layered clothing is ideal for spring and autumn, while summer requires lighter attire. In winter, warm clothing and waterproof gear are essential.

- Crowds and Prices: Summer is the busiest and most expensive time to cruise. For a more budget-friendly and less crowded experience, consider spring or autumn.

- Special Events: Plan your trip around special events and festivals for an enhanced experience. Booking early for popular events is advisable.

By choosing the right season for your Rhine River cruise, you'll ensure that your journey is not only enjoyable but also aligns with your interests and preferences. Each season offers its own unique charm, making the Rhine a year-round destination worth exploring.

Chapter 1: Preparing for Your Journey

Choosing the Right Cruise: Types and Options

Planning a Rhine River cruise is an exciting adventure, but with so many options available, it can be a bit overwhelming to choose the right one. Whether you're looking for luxury, budget-friendly, or themed cruises, there's something for everyone on the Rhine.

Luxury Cruises

Luxury cruises offer an unparalleled experience with top-notch amenities, gourmet dining, and exceptional service. Companies like Viking River Cruises and AmaWaterways are renowned for their luxurious ships, featuring spacious cabins, private balconies, and all-inclusive packages. These cruises often include guided shore excursions, wine tastings, and exclusive access to historical sites.

Budget-Friendly Cruises

If you're looking to explore the Rhine without breaking the bank, budget-friendly options are available too. Companies like CroisiEurope and Avalon Waterways offer affordable packages that still provide comfortable accommodations and delightful experiences. These cruises might not have all the bells and whistles of luxury liners, but they ensure you get to see the beautiful landscapes and historic sites along the Rhine.

Themed Cruises

For a unique experience, consider themed cruises. These can range from wine and culinary cruises to history and culture tours. For example, a wine-themed cruise might include visits to local vineyards, wine tastings, and lectures by sommeliers. A history-themed cruise could focus on medieval castles, ancient Roman sites, and museums along the route. These cruises are perfect for travelers with specific interests looking to deepen their knowledge and enjoy specialized activities.

Family-Friendly Cruises

Traveling with family? Many cruise lines offer family-friendly packages that cater to all ages. These cruises typically include kid-friendly activities, family excursions, and sometimes even babysitting services. Disney River Cruises, for instance, are known for their family-oriented experiences, combining the magic of Disney with the beauty of the Rhine.

Solo Traveler Cruises

For solo travelers, several cruise lines provide single cabins and social activities designed to help you connect with fellow travelers. Solo traveler cruises often feature group dinners, social events, and solo traveler meet-ups, ensuring you never feel alone on your journey.

Personal Experience

When I first embarked on a Rhine River cruise, I chose a themed wine cruise with AmaWaterways. The experience was incredible – from vineyard tours in the Rheingau region to wine tastings onboard, each day was filled with new and delightful experiences. The attention to detail and the quality of service made it a memorable trip, and I highly recommend themed cruises for those looking to indulge in their passions while traveling.

Booking Your Cruise: Tips and Tricks

Once you've decided on the type of cruise, it's time to book. Here are some tips and tricks to help you get the best deal and ensure a smooth booking process.

Book Early

Booking early is one of the best ways to secure your spot and get the best rates. Many cruise lines offer early-bird discounts and incentives for those who plan ahead. Additionally, booking early gives you a better selection of cabins and itineraries.

Look for Promotions and Discounts

Keep an eye out for promotions and discounts. Cruise lines frequently offer deals, such as discounted rates for groups, seniors, and solo travelers. Websites like Cruise Critic and Travelzoo can be great resources for finding these deals. Don't forget to sign up for newsletters from your preferred cruise lines to stay informed about upcoming promotions.

Consider Travel Insurance

Travel insurance is a wise investment for any trip, especially cruises. It can protect you from unexpected cancellations, medical emergencies, and lost luggage. Make sure to read the policy details carefully to understand what is covered.

Check Inclusions and Exclusions

When comparing cruise packages, pay attention to what's included and what's not. Some cruises are all-inclusive, covering meals, drinks, and excursions, while others might charge extra for these amenities. Understanding the full cost of your trip can help you avoid surprises and budget accordingly.

Flexible Dates

If your travel dates are flexible, you can often find better deals. Cruises during the shoulder seasons (spring and fall) tend to be less expensive than those in the peak summer months. Additionally, mid-week departures can sometimes be cheaper than weekend ones.

Use a Travel Agent

Travel agents can be a valuable resource when booking a cruise. They have access to exclusive deals, can provide expert advice, and help you navigate the booking process. Plus, their services are often free to the traveler, as they earn commissions from the cruise lines.

Personal Experience

During my first cruise booking, I found a fantastic deal through a travel agent. They were able to secure a discounted rate and even got us a complimentary cabin upgrade. Their insider knowledge and experience made the booking process smooth and stress-free, and I highly recommend using a travel agent for first-time cruisers.

Packing Essentials: What to Bring

Packing for a cruise requires careful planning to ensure you have everything you need for a comfortable and enjoyable trip. Here's a comprehensive list of essentials to bring on your Rhine River cruise.

Clothing

- Layered Clothing: The weather along the Rhine can vary, so pack layers that you can add or remove as needed. Lightweight sweaters, long-sleeve shirts, and jackets are ideal.

- Comfortable Shoes: You'll be doing a lot of walking during shore excursions, so bring comfortable walking shoes. Consider waterproof shoes or boots if you plan to hike or explore nature trails.

- Formal Wear: Some cruises have formal nights or special events, so pack at least one dressy outfit. For men, a suit or sports jacket and for women, a cocktail dress or dressy pantsuit.

- Casual Wear: Comfortable casual clothes for everyday wear onboard and during excursions.

- Swimwear: Many cruise ships have pools or spas, so bring a swimsuit if you plan to swim or relax in the hot tub.

Toiletries and Personal Care

- Toiletries: Toothbrush, toothpaste, shampoo, conditioner, soap, deodorant, and any other personal hygiene items.

- Sunscreen and Sunglasses: Protect yourself from the sun while enjoying the deck or exploring onshore.

- Medications: Bring any prescription medications, along with a basic first aid kit including pain relievers, motion sickness medication, and band-aids.

- Insect Repellent: Useful for excursions in nature.

Electronics and Gadgets

- Camera: Capture the stunning landscapes and memorable moments. Don't forget extra batteries and memory cards.

- Smartphone and Charger: Stay connected with family and friends, and use travel apps for navigation and information.

- Universal Power Adapter: Ensure you can charge your devices, especially if you're coming from outside Europe.

- Portable Power Bank: Keep your devices charged during long excursions.

Travel Documents and Money

- Passport and Visas: Ensure your passport is valid for at least six months beyond your travel dates. Check visa requirements for countries you'll be visiting.

- Cruise Tickets and Itinerary: Keep printed copies of your booking confirmation and itinerary.

- Travel Insurance Policy: Bring a copy of your travel insurance policy and emergency contact numbers.

- Cash and Credit Cards: Carry some local currency for small purchases and tips, and at least two credit cards for larger expenses.

Miscellaneous Items

- Daypack: A small backpack for carrying essentials during shore excursions.

- Reusable Water Bottle: Stay hydrated throughout your journey.

- Binoculars: Great for viewing distant landscapes and wildlife from the ship.

- Books or E-Reader: Enjoy some leisure reading during downtime.

- Snacks: Bring a few favorite snacks for late-night cravings or shore excursions.

Personal Experience

On my first Rhine River cruise, I underestimated the importance of comfortable shoes. After a full day of walking through the cobblestone streets of Strasbourg, my feet were sore and blistered. Now, I always pack a pair of well-broken-in walking shoes and a small first aid kit with blister pads. It made a world of difference on subsequent trips.

By choosing the right cruise, booking smartly, and packing thoughtfully, you'll be well-prepared for an unforgettable Rhine River cruise. Happy sailing!

Travel Documents and Health Precautions

Travel Documents: The Essentials

When embarking on your Rhine River cruise, ensuring you have all the necessary travel documents is crucial for a smooth and stress-free journey. Here's a detailed guide to help you navigate the essentials:

Passports and Visas:

Your passport is your most important travel document. Ensure that it is valid for at least six months beyond your planned return date. Some countries along the Rhine, such as Germany, France, and Switzerland, have specific entry requirements, so double-check if you need a visa. For most tourists from the US, Canada, and EU countries, a visa is not required for short stays.

Copies and Digital Backups:

Always make copies of your passport, visa, and other important documents. Keep one set of copies in your luggage and another with a trusted person back home. Additionally, save digital copies on a secure cloud service or email them to yourself for easy access in case of loss or theft.

Health Insurance and Travel Insurance:

Having comprehensive travel insurance is non-negotiable. It should cover medical expenses, trip cancellations, lost luggage, and any unexpected emergencies. Check if your health insurance policy covers international travel; if not, consider purchasing a policy that does. Trust me, having been in a situation where a travel companion fell ill abroad, the peace of mind from having insurance cannot be overstated.

Vaccination and Health Requirements:

While the Rhine region doesn't have specific vaccination requirements, it's always wise to stay updated on routine vaccines like MMR (measles, mumps, and rubella), diphtheria-tetanus-pertussis, and influenza. If you have specific health conditions, consult your doctor about any additional precautions you might need. Carry a basic first aid kit, along with any prescription medications you require, in their original packaging.

Emergency Contacts and Information:

Compile a list of emergency contacts, including local embassy numbers, medical facilities, and your travel insurance provider's hotline. Share your travel itinerary with family or friends so they can reach you in case of an emergency.

Budgeting Your Trip: Costs and Savings Tips

Budgeting Basics: Know Before You Go

A Rhine River cruise can range from luxurious to budget-friendly, depending on your choices. Here's how to plan your finances wisely:

Setting a Realistic Budget:

Start by determining your overall budget, considering all potential expenses. These include cruise fare, airfare, accommodations (if extending your stay), meals, excursions, tips, and souvenirs. Websites like CruiseCritic and TripAdvisor can help you gauge average costs.

Cruise Fare and Inclusions:

The cruise fare often includes accommodations, most meals, and some excursions. However, extras such as premium dining, special excursions, and spa treatments can add up. Look for all-inclusive packages to avoid unexpected costs. During a past cruise, opting for an all-inclusive deal saved me a lot of hassle and provided excellent value for money.

Airfare and Transfers:

Book your flights well in advance to secure the best deals. Use flight comparison websites like Skyscanner or Google Flights. Consider flying into a major hub like Amsterdam or Frankfurt, where flights are typically cheaper, and then taking a train to your departure port. Transfers from the airport to the cruise terminal are sometimes included, so verify with your cruise line.

Excursions and Sightseeing:

Pre-booking excursions can save you money and guarantee your spot on popular tours. Many cruise lines offer discounts for booking multiple excursions. Alternatively, consider independent tours or exploring on your own, which can be cheaper and more flexible. For example, during a stop in Strasbourg, I found a local walking tour that was half the price of the cruise line's offering and equally informative.

Meals and Dining:

While most meals are included, dining at specialty restaurants on the ship or sampling local cuisine at port stops can be an added expense. Set aside a portion of your budget for these experiences. Look for lunch specials or dine at local markets to enjoy authentic flavors without breaking the bank.

Tips and Gratuities:

Gratuities are often automatically added to your bill, but it's good practice to budget for additional tips for exceptional service. Research your cruise line's tipping policy in advance to avoid surprises.

Souvenirs and Shopping:

It's easy to get carried away with shopping. Set a budget for souvenirs and stick to it. Handmade crafts, local wines, and regional specialties make excellent gifts and mementos without costing a fortune.

Currency and Payment Methods:

The Rhine region uses the Euro, except in Switzerland, which uses the Swiss Franc. It's wise to have some local currency for small purchases. Credit cards are widely accepted, but notify your bank of your travel plans to avoid any issues. Consider using a travel credit card with no foreign transaction fees.

Savings Tips:

1. Early Booking Discounts: Many cruise lines offer significant discounts for early bookings. Plan and book your trip well in advance.

2. Off-Season Travel: Consider cruising during the shoulder seasons (spring and fall) when prices are lower, and the crowds are thinner.

3. Loyalty Programs: If you're a repeat cruiser, join loyalty programs for perks and discounts.

4. Group Rates: Traveling with family or friends? Look for group rates or discounts for booking multiple cabins.

By planning meticulously and budgeting smartly, you can enjoy your Rhine River cruise without financial stress, leaving you free to savor every moment of your journey.

Chapter 2: Itineraries and Route Plans

Overview of Popular Itineraries

Cruising the Rhine River offers a magical blend of history, culture, and natural beauty. Each bend in the river reveals new wonders, from ancient castles perched on hilltops to charming villages nestled along the riverbanks. Whether you're a first-time cruiser or a seasoned traveler, choosing the right itinerary can make all the difference in your experience. Here, we'll explore some of the most popular Rhine River cruise itineraries, giving you a taste of what each has to offer.

The Classic Rhine Cruise (Amsterdam to Basel)

The Classic Rhine Cruise is perhaps the most iconic and comprehensive route, typically spanning eight days. Starting in Amsterdam, the journey takes you through the heart of Europe, ending in Basel, Switzerland. This itinerary covers key cities like Cologne, Koblenz, and Strasbourg, offering a balanced mix of bustling urban centers and serene countryside.

Highlights:

- Amsterdam: Begin your journey in the vibrant capital of the Netherlands. Explore its famous canals, visit world-class museums like the Rijksmuseum, and indulge in the local cuisine.

- Cologne: Known for its stunning Gothic cathedral, Cologne is a blend of ancient history and modern energy. Don't miss the bustling Old Town and the chocolate museum.

- Koblenz: Situated at the confluence of the Rhine and Moselle rivers, Koblenz is a gateway to the Romantic Rhine. Visit the Deutsches Eck and take a cable car to Ehrenbreitstein Fortress.

- Rüdesheim: A quaint wine town famous for its Drosselgasse, a narrow alley lined with wine taverns. Enjoy a glass of local Riesling and visit the Siegfried's Mechanical Music Cabinet.

- Strasbourg: A beautiful city that straddles the border between France and Germany, known for its stunning cathedral and picturesque Petite France district.

- Basel: Conclude your cruise in this cultural Swiss city, renowned for its vibrant arts scene and historic old town.

The Romantic Rhine Cruise
(Mainz to Cologne)

For those with less time, the Romantic Rhine Cruise offers a shorter but equally enchanting journey, typically lasting four to five days. This route focuses on the most picturesque stretch of the Rhine, where castles, vineyards, and charming villages abound.

Highlights:

- Mainz: Start your trip in Mainz, a city steeped in history with a stunning cathedral and the Gutenberg Museum, dedicated to the inventor of the printing press.

- Rüdesheim: Enjoy the scenic beauty and wine culture of this charming town. Take a ride on the cable car for breathtaking views of the Rhine Valley.

- Bacharach: A quintessential medieval village with half-timbered houses and a serene ambiance. Explore its narrow streets and ancient churches.

- Lorelei Rock: Sail past the legendary Lorelei Rock, a steep slate rock on the right bank of the Rhine, associated with the myth of the enchanting siren.

- Koblenz: Visit the confluence of the Rhine and Moselle rivers and explore the historical monuments of this ancient city.

- Cologne: End your journey in Cologne, marveling at its iconic cathedral and vibrant cultural scene.

The Enchanted Rhine and Moselle Cruise (Amsterdam to Trier)

Combining the best of the Rhine and Moselle rivers, this extended itinerary, usually spanning ten to twelve days, offers an immersive experience into the heart of Europe's wine country.

Highlights:

- Amsterdam: Begin your adventure in the Dutch capital, enjoying its unique blend of history and modernity.

- Cologne: Discover the historical and cultural richness of Cologne.

- Koblenz: Explore the strategic city at the confluence of two major rivers.

- Cochem: Cruise along the Moselle River to the picturesque town of Cochem, known for its fairy-tale castle and excellent Riesling wines.

- Bernkastel-Kues: Another gem along the Moselle, famous for its medieval market square and world-class vineyards.

- Trier: End your journey in Trier, Germany's oldest city, with Roman ruins and a vibrant wine culture.

Detailed Day-by-Day Route Plans

Classic Rhine Cruise (Amsterdam to Basel)

Day 1: Amsterdam

- Morning: Arrive in Amsterdam and embark on your ship. Take some time to settle into your cabin.

- Afternoon: Explore the city's canals with a guided boat tour, visiting the Anne Frank House and the Rijksmuseum.

- Evening: Enjoy a welcome dinner onboard, followed by an evening stroll through Amsterdam's lively streets.

Day 2: Amsterdam to Cologne

- Morning: Enjoy breakfast as you sail towards Cologne. Attend an onboard lecture about the Rhine's history.

- Afternoon: Arrive in Cologne. Visit the Cologne Cathedral, a UNESCO World Heritage Site. Explore the Old Town and the Hohenzollern Bridge.

- Evening: Dine at a local restaurant or onboard. Optional excursion to a local brewery for a Kölsch beer tasting.

Day 3: Cologne to Koblenz

- Morning: Scenic cruising towards Koblenz. Enjoy views of castles and vineyards along the way.

- Afternoon: Arrive in Koblenz. Visit the Deutsches Eck and take the cable car to Ehrenbreitstein Fortress. Optional guided tour of the city.

- Evening: Dinner onboard with a view of the illuminated fortress.

Day 4: Koblenz to Rüdesheim

- Morning: Depart for Rüdesheim, sailing through the picturesque Middle Rhine Valley, a UNESCO World Heritage Site.

- Afternoon: Arrive in Rüdesheim. Explore the Drosselgasse and visit a local vineyard for a wine tasting.

- Evening: Enjoy a traditional German dinner and live music at a local tavern.

Day 5: Rüdesheim to Heidelberg

- Morning: Cruise towards Heidelberg. Attend a cooking demonstration onboard, featuring regional dishes.

- Afternoon: Arrive in Heidelberg. Visit the Heidelberg Castle and take a guided tour of the historic old town.

- Evening: Dinner onboard with scenic views of the Neckar River.

Day 6: Heidelberg to Strasbourg

- Morning: Depart for Strasbourg. Participate in a wine and cheese pairing session onboard.

- Afternoon: Arrive in Strasbourg. Explore the city's cathedral and Petite France district on a guided tour.

- Evening: Enjoy Alsatian cuisine at a local restaurant or onboard.

Day 7: Strasbourg to Basel

- Morning: Scenic cruising towards Basel. Relax and enjoy the views or join a yoga session on deck.

- Afternoon: Arrive in Basel. Visit the Kunstmuseum and explore the old town.

- Evening: Farewell dinner onboard, celebrating the end of your journey.

Day 8: Basel

- Morning: Disembark after breakfast. Optional post-cruise extensions to Zurich or Lucerne.

Romantic Rhine Cruise (Mainz to Cologne)

Day 1: Mainz

- Morning: Embark in Mainz. Visit the Mainz Cathedral and the Gutenberg Museum.

- Afternoon: Explore the old town, with its charming squares and half-timbered houses.

- Evening: Welcome dinner onboard, followed by a leisurely walk along the riverbank.

Day 2: Mainz to Rüdesheim

- Morning: Scenic cruising towards Rüdesheim. Attend a lecture on Rhine Valley wines.

- Afternoon: Arrive in Rüdesheim. Ride the cable car for panoramic views and visit Siegfried's Mechanical Music Cabinet.

- Evening: Dinner at a local wine tavern, enjoying traditional German music.

Day 3: Rüdesheim to Koblenz

- Morning: Sail past the Lorelei Rock. Learn about the legends surrounding this iconic site.

- Afternoon: Arrive in Koblenz. Explore the Deutsches Eck and take a walking tour of the old town.

- Evening: Dinner onboard, followed by an optional night tour of the city.

Day 4: Koblenz to Cologne

- Morning: Cruise towards Cologne. Attend an onboard cooking class, learning to make local dishes.

- Afternoon: Arrive in Cologne. Visit the Cologne Cathedral and the Roman-Germanic Museum.

- Evening: Farewell dinner onboard. Optional evening cruise to see the city lights.

Day 5: Cologne

- Morning: Disembark after breakfast. Optional city tour or extension to nearby attractions.

By following these detailed itineraries, you can ensure that every moment of your Rhine River cruise is filled with discovery, relaxation, and unforgettable experiences. Whether you're marveling at the Gothic spires of Cologne Cathedral or savoring a glass of Riesling in Rüdesheim, each day promises new adventures and lasting memories.

Customizable Itinerary Options

Planning a Rhine River cruise is an exciting adventure, and one of the best parts is customizing your itinerary to suit your interests and preferences. Whether you love history, culture, food, or nature, there's something along the Rhine for everyone. Here are some customizable itinerary options to consider, ensuring your cruise is uniquely tailored to your desires.

Option 1: The Historical Explorer

Day 1: Amsterdam

- Morning: Visit the Anne Frank House for a poignant reminder of history.

- Afternoon: Explore the Rijksmuseum to admire works by Rembrandt and Vermeer.

- Evening: Enjoy a canal cruise to see the city's stunning architecture lit up at night.

Day 2: Cologne

- Morning: Start with a tour of the Cologne Cathedral, a Gothic masterpiece.

- Afternoon: Visit the Romano-Germanic Museum to dive into the city's ancient past.

- Evening: Walk along the Rhine promenade, enjoying the views and vibrant atmosphere.

Day 3: Koblenz

- Morning: Take a cable car to Ehrenbreitstein Fortress for panoramic views.

- Afternoon: Wander through the historic old town and visit the Deutsches Eck.

- Evening: Relax in a local café with a view of the confluence of the Rhine and Moselle rivers.

Day 4: Rüdesheim

- Morning: Tour Siegfried's Mechanical Music Cabinet, a quirky museum of automated instruments.

- Afternoon: Stroll along the Drosselgasse, a charming street filled with shops and wine taverns.

- Evening: Enjoy a wine tasting at a local vineyard, sampling the renowned Rheingau wines.

Day 5: Heidelberg

- Morning: Explore Heidelberg Castle, with its rich history and stunning views.

- Afternoon: Walk along the Philosopher's Walk for breathtaking views of the city and the Neckar River.

- Evening: Dine at a traditional German restaurant, savoring local specialties.

Day 6: Strasbourg

- Morning: Visit the Strasbourg Cathedral and climb the tower for a magnificent view.

- Afternoon: Wander through La Petite France, a picturesque district with half-timbered houses.

- Evening: Enjoy a dinner cruise along the Ill River, taking in the illuminated cityscape.

Day 7: Basel

- Morning: Visit the Kunstmuseum Basel, home to an impressive collection of art.

- Afternoon: Explore the old town, with its medieval buildings and bustling market squares.

- Evening: End your journey with a gourmet meal at a Michelin-starred restaurant.

Option 2: The Nature Lover

Day 1: Amsterdam

- Morning: Start with a visit to the Keukenhof Gardens (if in season) to see stunning tulip displays.

- Afternoon: Take a bike tour of the countryside, exploring windmills and charming villages.

- Evening: Relax on a sunset canal cruise, enjoying the serene waterways.

Day 2: Cologne

- Morning: Explore the Botanical Gardens Flora, a green oasis in the city.

- Afternoon: Take a leisurely walk along the Rhine River, enjoying the scenic views.

- Evening: Visit a local beer garden to sample Kölsch beer and regional dishes.

Day 3: Koblenz

- Morning: Hike the trails around Ehrenbreitstein Fortress, offering beautiful vistas.

- Afternoon: Enjoy a boat ride to Marksburg Castle, a well-preserved medieval fortress.

- Evening: Stroll through the old town and along the riverside promenade.

Day 4: Rüdesheim

- Morning: Take a cable car ride over the vineyards to the Niederwald Monument.

- Afternoon: Hike through the Rheingau region, stopping at scenic overlooks.

- Evening: Indulge in a wine tasting session at a local winery.

Day 5: Heidelberg

- Morning: Explore the Heidelberg Botanical Garden, one of the oldest in Germany.

- Afternoon: Take a river cruise on the Neckar, surrounded by lush hills and historic castles.

- Evening: Walk along the Neckarwiese, a riverside park perfect for a relaxing evening.

Day 6: Strasbourg

- Morning: Discover the Orangerie Park, a beautiful green space with lakes and gardens.

- Afternoon: Take a boat tour of the canals, offering unique views of the city's architecture.

- Evening: Enjoy a picnic dinner in one of the city's many parks.

Day 7: Basel

- Morning: Visit the Basel Zoo, known for its diverse collection of animals.

- Afternoon: Hike the nearby Jura Mountains, offering stunning landscapes and panoramic views.

- Evening: Conclude your journey with a scenic dinner at a restaurant overlooking the Rhine.

Tips for Maximizing Your Time at Each Stop

Maximizing your time at each stop along the Rhine River ensures you get the most out of your cruise experience. Here are some tips to help you make the most of your visits:

1. Plan Ahead

   - Research each destination before your trip and prioritize the must-see attractions.

   - Book any necessary tickets or tours in advance to avoid long lines and ensure availability.

2. Start Early

   - Begin your day early to beat the crowds and have more time to explore.

   - Mornings are often quieter, allowing you to enjoy popular sites with fewer tourists.

3. Use Efficient Transportation

   - Take advantage of local transportation options, such as trams, buses, and bikes, to get around quickly.

- Consider using hop-on-hop-off bus tours for a convenient way to see multiple attractions.

4. Combine Activities

- Look for ways to combine activities, such as a walking tour that includes visits to several key sites.

- Many cities offer combination tickets for multiple attractions, saving you time and money.

5. Stay Flexible

- Be open to adjusting your plans based on weather, local events, or personal preferences.

- Sometimes the best experiences come from spontaneous decisions.

6. Take Guided Tours

- Join guided tours to gain deeper insights into the history and culture of each destination.

- Guides can provide valuable tips and help you navigate efficiently.

7. Pack Light

- Carry only what you need for the day to stay comfortable and mobile.

- Use a small backpack or bag for essentials like water, snacks, and a camera.

8. Use Technology

- Utilize travel apps for maps, public transportation schedules, and local recommendations.

- Audio guides and virtual tours can enhance your experience at historical sites and museums.

9. Engage with Locals

- Interact with local residents to get insider tips and recommendations.

- Dining at local restaurants and visiting markets can provide a more authentic experience.

10. Take Breaks

- Allow time for breaks to rest and recharge, especially if you're walking or biking a lot.

- Enjoy a coffee or a snack at a local café while people-watching and soaking in the atmosphere.

By following these tips, you can ensure that each stop on your Rhine River cruise is enjoyable, enriching, and memorable.

Chapter 3: Key Destinations and Stopovers

Amsterdam: The Journey Begins

Amsterdam, the vibrant capital of the Netherlands, is often the starting point for many Rhine River cruises. Its picturesque canals, rich history, and lively culture make it an unforgettable beginning to your journey. Let's dive into what makes Amsterdam a must-visit destination.

A City of Canals and Culture

As you arrive in Amsterdam, the first thing you'll notice is its iconic network of canals. These waterways, dating back to the 17th century, are not just a means of transportation but a UNESCO World Heritage site. Taking a canal cruise is an ideal way to start your exploration. Glide through the serene waters, passing under charming bridges and alongside gabled houses that tell stories of a bygone era.

Historical Treasures

Amsterdam is a city steeped in history. The Anne Frank House is one of the most poignant historical sites you can visit. Walking through the rooms where Anne Frank and her family hid during World War II is a deeply moving experience. The preserved diary entries offer a window into the past that leaves a lasting impact on every visitor.

Another historical gem is the Rijksmuseum, home to masterpieces by Dutch artists like Rembrandt and Vermeer. The museum's vast collection spans over 800 years of art and history, providing an enriching experience for art lovers and history buffs alike.

The Charm of the Jordaan District

For a taste of local life, stroll through the Jordaan district. Once a working-class neighborhood, Jordaan is now one of Amsterdam's most desirable areas, filled with independent boutiques, cozy cafes, and vibrant street markets. The Noordermarkt, held on Saturdays, is perfect for sampling local delicacies and finding unique souvenirs.

Culinary Delights

Amsterdam's food scene is as diverse as its population. From traditional Dutch pancakes (pannenkoeken) to exotic Indonesian rijsttafel, there's something to satisfy every palate. Don't miss out on trying stroopwafels, a delightful Dutch treat made of two thin waffles with a caramel syrup filling. You can find the freshest ones at Albert Cuyp Market.

Engaging Activities

Amsterdam offers a plethora of activities for every type of traveler. Rent a bike and explore the city like a local, as Amsterdam is one of the most bike-friendly cities in the world. Visit the Van Gogh Museum to marvel at the largest collection of Van Gogh's works, or take a relaxing stroll through Vondelpark, the city's most famous park.

Cologne: A Blend of History and Modernity

As your cruise glides into Germany, Cologne emerges as a captivating blend of history and modernity. Known for its impressive cathedral and vibrant cultural scene, Cologne offers a rich tapestry of experiences.

The Majestic Cologne Cathedral

The Cologne Cathedral, a UNESCO World Heritage site, dominates the skyline and is a marvel of Gothic architecture. Its twin spires, soaring 157 meters into the sky, are an iconic symbol of the city. Inside, the cathedral is just as impressive, with stunning stained glass windows and the Shrine of the

Three Kings, said to contain relics of the Magi. Climb the 533 steps to the top for a breathtaking panoramic view of the city.

A Walk Through History

Cologne's history dates back to Roman times, and evidence of this ancient past can be found throughout the city. The Roman-Germanic Museum, located near the cathedral, houses an extensive collection of Roman artifacts, including the famous Dionysus mosaic. Walking through its exhibits, you get a sense of the city's importance during the Roman Empire.

Modern Marvels and Shopping

While Cologne is rich in history, it also embraces the present with a vibrant modern culture. The city's shopping streets, particularly Schildergasse and Hohe Strasse, are bustling with activity and offer everything from high-end fashion to quirky boutiques. The Rheinauhafen district is a testament to modern architecture, with its distinctive crane houses and trendy restaurants.

Cultural Delights

Cologne is also known for its lively cultural scene. The Museum Ludwig, adjacent to the cathedral, is home to one of the largest collections of modern art in Europe, featuring works by Picasso, Warhol, and Lichtenstein. For a more local flavor, visit the Fragrance Museum, which tells the story of Eau de Cologne, the city's most famous export.

Culinary Adventures

No visit to Cologne is complete without sampling its culinary offerings. The city is famous for its Kölsch beer, served in small, straight glasses at traditional beer halls like Früh am Dom. Pair your beer with hearty German dishes like . Himmel un Ääd (mashed potatoes with apples and black pudding) or Rievkooche (potato pancakes).

For a sweeter treat, try a piece of local chocolate from the Chocolate Museum, which not only offers tastings but also provides an insightful look into the history and production of chocolate.

Festivals and Events

Cologne hosts numerous festivals throughout the year, with the Cologne Carnival being the most famous. This vibrant celebration, often referred to as the "fifth season," features parades, costumes, and street parties, drawing visitors from all over the world. Whether you're in Cologne for the carnival or another time of year, there's always something happening in this dynamic city.

Koblenz: Gateway to the Romantic Rhine

Koblenz is a charming city that sits at the confluence of the Rhine and Moselle rivers, offering a unique blend of natural beauty and rich history. As the gateway to the Romantic Rhine, Koblenz is a must-visit destination on any Rhine River cruise.

A Journey Through History

Walking through Koblenz feels like stepping back in time. The city's history dates back over 2,000 years, and this long past is evident in its well-preserved architecture and historical landmarks. One of the most iconic sites is the Deutsches Eck, or German Corner, where a grand equestrian statue of Emperor William I stands guard over the point where the two rivers meet. This is not just a beautiful spot for a photo; it's a place steeped in the unity of the German states.

Nearby, you'll find the Ehrenbreitstein Fortress, a massive fortification perched high on a hill overlooking the Rhine. This fortress, which is one of the largest preserved fortresses in Europe, offers stunning panoramic views of the river and the surrounding landscape. Take the cable car from the riverside to the fortress for a scenic and thrilling ascent.

Cultural Delights

Koblenz is also a city of vibrant culture. The Middle Rhine Museum and the Ludwig Museum offer art and history enthusiasts a wealth of exhibits to explore. The Middle Rhine Museum focuses on the cultural history of the region, while the Ludwig Museum is renowned for its contemporary art collections.

If you visit during the summer, you might be lucky enough to experience the Rhine in Flames festival, a spectacular event where fireworks light up the night sky, synchronized with music. This festival is a true celebration of the Rhine and an unforgettable experience for any visitor.

Strolling and Shopping

The old town of Koblenz is perfect for a leisurely stroll. Its cobbled streets are lined with quaint shops, cozy cafes, and traditional restaurants. Be sure to visit the Jesuitenplatz, a picturesque square surrounded by historic buildings, where you can enjoy a cup of coffee and watch the world go by.

Personal Tip: When in Koblenz, don't miss trying the local wine. The Rhine and Moselle regions are famous for their wines, particularly Rieslings. Many local restaurants offer wine tastings, providing the perfect opportunity to sample some of the finest vintages.

Rüdesheim: Wine and Dine

Rüdesheim is a picturesque town known for its wine and its charming, medieval atmosphere. Nestled in the heart of the Rhine Gorge, Rüdesheim offers a perfect blend of scenic beauty, cultural heritage, and gastronomic delights.

Wine Lover's Paradise

Rüdesheim is synonymous with wine. The town is surrounded by vineyards, and wine production is a way of life here. The Drosselgasse, a narrow, cobbled street in the heart of the town, is famous for its wine taverns. This lively street, just 144 meters long, is packed with traditional taverns, each offering its own unique selection of local wines.

Take a seat at one of these cozy taverns and enjoy a glass of Riesling or Spätburgunder while listening to live folk music. The atmosphere is always vibrant, especially in the evenings when the street comes alive with both locals and tourists.

Exploring the Vineyards

For a more immersive wine experience, visit the vineyards themselves. Many local wineries offer tours and tastings, where you can learn about the winemaking process and sample a variety of wines directly from the source. One of the most popular is the Weingut Georg Breuer, known for its exquisite Rieslings. A vineyard tour here provides not only great wine but also breathtaking views of the Rhine Valley.

Historical Highlights

Beyond its wines, Rüdesheim is rich in history. The Siegfried's Mechanical Music Cabinet is a fascinating museum dedicated to mechanical musical instruments. The museum, housed in a historic castle, features an impressive collection of self-playing pianos, music boxes, and other mechanical wonders from the 18th and 19th centuries. It's a delightful experience that combines music, history, and engineering.

Scenic Views and Cable Cars

For panoramic views of the Rhine, take the cable car up to the Niederwald Monument. This impressive monument, built to commemorate the unification of Germany, offers stunning views over the vineyards and the river. The ride itself is a highlight, providing a bird's eye view of the beautiful landscape below.

Culinary Delights

Rüdesheim's culinary scene is just as impressive as its wine. Traditional German dishes like sausages, pretzels, and schnitzels are staples, but the town also boasts unique local specialties. Be sure to try the Rüdesheimer Kaffee, a delightful coffee drink made with locally distilled Asbach brandy, sugar, and whipped cream.

Personal Tip: For a truly memorable meal, dine at one of the town's riverside restaurants. Enjoying a meal with a view of the Rhine, especially at sunset, is an experience you'll cherish.

Festivals and Events

Rüdesheim hosts several festivals throughout the year, celebrating everything from wine to Christmas. The Rüdesheim Wine Festival, held in August, is a fantastic opportunity to sample a wide range of wines and enjoy live music and entertainment. The town's Christmas Market of Nations, held during the holiday season, is a magical event where the streets are transformed with festive decorations, and stalls offer crafts and foods from around the world.

Personal Reflections

Having traveled to both Koblenz and Rüdesheim, I can attest to the unique charm and allure of each town. Koblenz's historical significance and vibrant culture make it a fascinating destination, while Rüdesheim's focus on wine and its picturesque setting create an enchanting experience. Each town offers something special, ensuring that your Rhine River cruise will be filled with memorable moments.

Whether you're exploring ancient fortresses, sampling exquisite wines, or simply soaking in the scenic beauty of the Rhine Valley, these stops on your cruise will undoubtedly leave a lasting impression. So raise a glass, take in the views, and enjoy the incredible journey that the Rhine has to offer.

Heidelberg: Romantic and Historic

Nestled in the heart of Germany, Heidelberg is a city that oozes romance and history at every turn. As you step off the cruise and onto its charming cobblestone streets, you'll quickly understand why this city has inspired poets, artists, and scholars for centuries. The enchanting blend of old-world charm and vibrant modernity makes Heidelberg an unmissable stop on your Rhine River journey.

Exploring Heidelberg Castle: A Majestic Ruin

Your visit to Heidelberg wouldn't be complete without a trip to its iconic castle. Perched on Königstuhl hill, the Heidelberg Castle offers panoramic views of the city and the Neckar River. This stunning structure, a mix of Gothic and Renaissance architecture, tells tales of grandeur and destruction. Stroll through the castle gardens, explore the ruins, and don't miss the Great Tun – one of the largest wine barrels in the world!

The Philosopher's Walk: A Path of Inspiration

For a truly unique experience, take a leisurely walk along the Philosopher's Walk (Philosophenweg). This scenic path, which winds through vineyards and wooded hills, was a favorite spot for Heidelberg's scholars. The walk offers breathtaking views of the city and the castle, making it a perfect place for contemplation and photography.

The Old Bridge: A Historic Gateway

Crossing the Neckar River, the Old Bridge (Alte Brücke) connects the old town to the Neuenheim district. Built in the 18th century, this stone bridge is adorned with statues and offers a picturesque setting for a leisurely stroll. As you cross, take a moment to admire the charming bridge gate and the serene river views.

Heidelberg University: A Hub of Knowledge

Heidelberg is home to Germany's oldest university, founded in 1386. A visit to Heidelberg University gives you a glimpse into the city's academic legacy. Wander through the historic buildings, including the Old University and the University Library. Don't miss the Student Jail (Studentenkarzer), where misbehaving students were once confined – it's now a quirky museum filled with graffiti and tales of student life from the past.

The Altstadt: Heart of the Old Town

The Altstadt, or Old Town, is the vibrant heart of Heidelberg. Here, narrow lanes are lined with beautifully preserved Baroque buildings, inviting cafes, and boutique shops. The Marktplatz, the main square, is a perfect place to soak in the local atmosphere. Grab a seat at a café, sip on a cup of rich German coffee, and watch the world go by.

Dining in Heidelberg: A Culinary Delight

Heidelberg's culinary scene is as diverse as its history. For a traditional German meal, head to one of the many rustic taverns in the Old Town. Savor hearty dishes like Sauerbraten (pot roast) or Käsespätzle (cheese noodles), paired with a local beer or a glass of wine from the nearby Pfalz region. For dessert, don't miss the opportunity to try a slice of the famous Schwarzwälder Kirschtorte (Black Forest cake).

Strasbourg: A Taste of France

Crossing into France, your Rhine River cruise brings you to Strasbourg, a city where French and German influences blend seamlessly. Strasbourg's unique charm lies in its picturesque canals, half-timbered houses, and a rich cultural tapestry that offers a taste of both nations.

La Petite France: A Fairytale District

La Petite France is Strasbourg's most enchanting district. This UNESCO World Heritage site is a maze of narrow streets, canals, and beautifully preserved half-timbered houses. Wander along the cobblestone lanes, take a boat tour through the canals, and soak in the fairy-tale ambiance. The area is particularly magical at sunset, when the buildings reflect in the water, creating a scene straight out of a storybook.

Strasbourg Cathedral: A Gothic Masterpiece

Dominating the city's skyline, the Strasbourg Cathedral (Cathédrale Notre-Dame de Strasbourg) is a marvel of Gothic architecture. Its intricate façade, adorned with thousands of sculptures, will leave you in awe. Step inside to admire the stunning stained-glass windows and the astronomical clock, a masterpiece of engineering and artistry. Climb the cathedral's tower for panoramic views of the city and the Rhine River.

European Quarter: A Hub of Politics and Culture

Strasbourg is not only a historical gem but also a center of European politics. The European Quarter is home to several important institutions, including the European Parliament and the Council of Europe. Take a guided tour to learn about the workings of these institutions and their impact on European integration.

The Alsatian Cuisine: A Fusion of Flavors

Strasbourg's culinary scene is a delightful blend of French finesse and German heartiness. Treat yourself to a traditional Alsatian meal at a winstub (a cozy wine tavern). Indulge in dishes like Choucroute garnie (sauerkraut with sausages and pork) and Tarte flambée (a thin-crust pizza-like dish topped with crème fraîche, onions, and bacon). Pair your meal with a glass of local Riesling or Gewürztraminer, wines that perfectly complement the region's cuisine.

Exploring the Grand Île: The Heart of Strasbourg

The Grand Île, Strasbourg's historic center, is an island surrounded by the Ill River. This area is packed with cultural and architectural treasures. Wander through Place Kléber, the city's main square, and visit the nearby Palais Rohan, a grand palace housing three museums. Stroll along the Rue des Orfèvres, a charming street lined with boutiques and artisanal shops.

The Covered Bridges and Barrage Vauban: Engineering Marvels

A short walk from La Petite France, you'll find the Covered Bridges (Ponts Couverts) and the Barrage Vauban. These 17th-century defensive structures are engineering marvels that offer a fascinating glimpse into Strasbourg's past. Walk along the covered walkways for stunning views of the canals and the cityscape.

Festivals and Events: Celebrating Culture and Heritage

Strasbourg is a city that loves to celebrate. If you visit during the holiday season, the Strasbourg Christmas Market is a must-see. As one of the oldest and most famous Christmas markets in Europe, it transforms the city into a winter wonderland. Throughout the year, Strasbourg hosts numerous festivals, from the classical music extravaganza of the Strasbourg Music Festival to the contemporary art showcase of the St-art Fair.

Heidelberg and Strasbourg are two captivating stops on your Rhine River cruise, each offering its own unique blend of history, culture, and charm. Whether you're exploring ancient castles, strolling through fairy-tale streets, or indulging in local culinary delights, these cities promise unforgettable experiences that will make your journey along the Rhine truly special. So, get ready to immerse yourself in the romance of Heidelberg and the multicultural charm of Strasbourg – two destinations that will capture your heart and imagination.

Basel: The Cultural Capital of Switzerland

Nestled at the meeting point of Switzerland, France, and Germany, Basel is a city that effortlessly blends a rich historical past with vibrant contemporary culture. This cosmopolitan city, often overlooked by travelers, stands as a beacon of art, architecture, and innovation along the banks of the Rhine River. Let's embark on a detailed exploration of Basel, a city that promises a fascinating journey through time and creativity.

1. A Historical Tapestry: From Ancient Roots to Modern Marvels

Basel's history stretches back to the days of the Roman Empire, and its strategic location made it a significant hub for trade and culture. The city's old town, with its cobblestone streets and medieval buildings, offers a glimpse into its storied past. As you wander through the winding alleys, you'll encounter beautifully preserved architecture, from the imposing Basel Minster to the charming Spalentor gate.

Basel Minster: This Gothic cathedral, with its striking red sandstone façade and twin towers, dominates the city's skyline. Originally built between the 12th and 15th centuries, the Minster offers panoramic views of Basel and the Rhine from its towers. The interior is equally captivating, featuring intricate stained glass windows and a crypt dating back to the 10th century.

Spalentor Gate: One of the most beautiful gates of the old city walls, Spalentor stands as a testament to Basel's medieval fortifications. Built in the 14th century, this gate is adorned with impressive sculptures and offers a picturesque entry point to the old town.

2. A Mecca for Art Enthusiasts: Museums and Galleries

Basel is often hailed as the cultural capital of Switzerland, and for good reason. The city is home to an astounding number of museums and galleries, making it a paradise for art lovers. Whether you're interested in classical masterpieces or cutting-edge contemporary art, Basel's cultural offerings will leave you spellbound.

Kunstmuseum Basel: Renowned as the oldest public art collection in the world, the Kunstmuseum houses an impressive array of works spanning from the Middle Ages to modern times. Here, you can admire pieces by Holbein, Picasso, and Van Gogh, among many others. The museum's modern extension, completed in 2016, seamlessly blends old and new, offering a fresh perspective on its extensive collection.

Fondation Beyeler: Located just outside the city in Riehen, the Fondation Beyeler is one of Switzerland's most visited museums. Designed by the celebrated architect Renzo Piano, the museum showcases an extraordinary collection of modern and contemporary art. Works by Monet, Cézanne, and Rothko are displayed in a serene setting that harmonizes with the surrounding landscape.

Museum Tinguely: Dedicated to the life and work of the Swiss artist Jean Tinguely, this museum offers a playful exploration of kinetic art. Tinguely's whimsical, moving sculptures captivate visitors of all ages, making it a must-visit for families.

3. Architectural Wonders: A Fusion of Old and New

Basel's architecture is a fascinating mix of medieval, Renaissance, and modern styles. The city's commitment to innovative design is evident in its skyline, where historic buildings stand shoulder to shoulder with contemporary masterpieces.

Vitra Campus: Just a short trip from Basel, the Vitra Campus in Weil am Rhein, Germany, is an architectural enthusiast's dream. Featuring buildings by renowned architects such as Frank Gehry, Zaha Hadid, and Herzog & de Meuron, the campus is both a working furniture factory and a design museum. The VitraHaus, designed by Herzog & de Meuron, offers a unique retail experience with a stunning display of Vitra's furniture.

Tinguely Fountain: Located outside the Basel Theatre, this playful fountain was designed by Jean Tinguely. The mechanical sculptures within the fountain move and spray water, creating a delightful spectacle that reflects Tinguely's signature style.

Basel's Town Hall (Rathaus): With its vibrant red façade and richly decorated exterior, the Town Hall is a standout landmark in the city. The building's interior courtyard is equally impressive, adorned with murals depicting historical scenes.

4. Culinary Delights: A Taste of Basel

No visit to Basel would be complete without indulging in its culinary offerings. The city's diverse food scene reflects its multicultural heritage, offering everything from traditional Swiss dishes to international cuisine.

Local Specialties: Be sure to try Basler Läckerli, a traditional hard gingerbread made with honey, almonds, candied peel, and Kirsch. This sweet treat has been a Basel specialty since the 15th century. Another must-try is the Zwiebelwähe, a savory onion tart that's perfect for a quick snack.

Fine Dining: For a memorable dining experience, visit Cheval Blanc by Peter Knogl, a three-Michelin-star restaurant located in the Grand Hotel Les Trois Rois. The menu here is a fusion of French haute cuisine and Mediterranean influences, with each dish meticulously crafted to delight the senses.

Markets and Street Food: The Marktplatz in the heart of the old town is home to a vibrant market where you can sample local produce, cheeses, and baked goods. During the festive season, the Basel Christmas Market is a magical place to enjoy seasonal treats and warm mulled wine.

5. Festivals and Events: Celebrating Basel's Vibrant Culture

Basel's cultural calendar is packed with events and festivals that draw visitors from around the world. Here are some highlights you won't want to miss:

Basel Carnival (Fasnacht): Known as the largest carnival in Switzerland, Fasnacht is a colorful three-day event that takes place in February or March. The streets of Basel come alive with music, parades, and elaborate costumes, creating an atmosphere of joyous celebration.

Art Basel: This prestigious art fair, held annually in June, attracts artists, collectors, and enthusiasts from across the globe. Art Basel showcases contemporary art in various forms, from paintings and sculptures to installations and digital art.

Basel Tattoo: Every July, Basel hosts one of the world's largest military music festivals. The Basel Tattoo features performances by military bands and display teams from around the world, set against the backdrop of the historic Kaserne.

Basel is a city that truly has something for everyone. Whether you're an art aficionado, a history buff, or a foodie, you'll find endless opportunities for exploration and enjoyment. With its rich cultural heritage, stunning architecture, and vibrant events, Basel is a destination that promises an unforgettable experience. So, as you cruise along the Rhine, make sure to immerse yourself in the wonders of Basel, the cultural heart of Switzerland.

Chapter 4: Hidden Gems and Secret Treasures

Exploring the Rhine River is like stepping into a fairy tale, with its majestic castles, charming villages, and serene landscapes. While the popular destinations are well-known for a reason, there are numerous lesser-known gems and off-the-beaten-path attractions that offer a unique and enriching experience. This chapter will guide you through some of these hidden treasures, ensuring that your journey along the Rhine is filled with delightful surprises.

Lesser-Known Villages to Explore

1. Bacharach: A Timeless Beauty

Nestled in the heart of the Rhine Gorge, Bacharach is a picturesque village that seems to have been frozen in time. Known for its half-timbered houses and cobblestone streets, Bacharach offers a tranquil escape from the hustle and bustle of more tourist-heavy spots.

Stroll through the village, and you'll discover Stahleck Castle, perched high above the Rhine, now a youth hostel with stunning views. The Church of St. Peter, with its striking red and white façade, stands as a testament to the village's medieval past. Don't miss the Postenturm, an ancient watchtower offering panoramic vistas of the surrounding vineyards and river.

2. Oberwesel: The Town of Towers

Oberwesel, often overshadowed by nearby St. Goar, is a hidden gem that boasts more than just its famous Schönburg Castle. Known as the "Town of Towers," Oberwesel's skyline is dotted with medieval fortifications that transport you back to the days of knights and legends.

A walk along the old town wall, which still encircles the town, reveals well-preserved towers and gates. The Liebfrauenkirche (Church of Our Lady) is a Gothic masterpiece with beautiful stained glass windows. For wine enthusiasts, Oberwesel's vineyards produce some of the finest Rieslings in the region, and a visit to a local winery for a tasting is a must.

3. Boppard: A Riverside Haven

While Boppard may not be as obscure as other villages, it often gets overlooked in favor of larger towns. This charming riverside haven offers a perfect blend of natural beauty and historical intrigue. The town's Roman history is evident in its ruins, and the medieval architecture adds to its charm.

Take the chairlift up to Gedeonseck for breathtaking views of the Rhine loop, a unique bend in the river that is one of the most photographed spots in the region. The town's promenade is perfect for a leisurely stroll, and its numerous cafes and restaurants offer a taste of local cuisine.

Off-the-Beaten-Path Attractions

1. Marksburg Castle: A Medieval Fortress

Unlike many of the castles along the Rhine, Marksburg Castle has never been destroyed, making it one of the best-preserved medieval fortresses in Germany. Located near the village of Braubach, this castle offers a fascinating glimpse into the past.

Visitors can explore the castle's various rooms, including the armory, the wine cellar, and the knights' hall. The castle also hosts medieval-themed events and reenactments, providing an immersive historical experience. The views from the castle's ramparts are nothing short of spectacular, offering sweeping vistas of the Rhine Valley.

2. The Lorelei Rock: Myth and Legend

The Lorelei Rock, near the town of St. Goarshausen, is shrouded in myth and legend. According to folklore, the rock was home to a beautiful siren named Lorelei, whose singing lured sailors to their doom on the treacherous waters below.

A visit to the Lorelei Rock offers more than just a scenic view; it's a cultural experience steeped in local lore. The Lorelei Visitor Center provides insight into the legend and the geology of the region. Hike up to the viewing platform for a panoramic view of the Rhine and the surrounding cliffs, and you'll understand why this spot has inspired poets and artists for centuries.

3. Rheinfels Castle: Ruins with a View

While not as intact as Marksburg, Rheinfels Castle in St. Goar is one of the largest and most imposing castle ruins on the Rhine. Built in the 13th century, the castle was a formidable fortress in its heyday.

Today, visitors can explore the extensive ruins, including the tunnels, dungeons, and the remnants of the keep. The castle museum provides historical context and houses artifacts from the medieval period. The views from Rheinfels are arguably the best along the Middle Rhine, offering a commanding panorama of the river and the valley below.

4. Pfalzgrafenstein Castle: The Toll Station of the Rhine

Pfalzgrafenstein Castle, located on a small island in the middle of the Rhine near Kaub, is often referred to as the "toll station of the Rhine." This unique castle, shaped like a ship, was used to collect tolls from passing vessels.

Accessible only by boat, a visit to Pfalzgrafenstein offers a unique perspective on the river's history. The castle's interior is well-preserved, with rooms that showcase the living conditions of the past. Standing on the castle's ramparts, surrounded by the river, gives you a sense of the strategic importance of this tiny fortress.

5. The Painted Houses of Linz am Rhein

Linz am Rhein, known as the "Colorful Town on the Rhine," is famous for its brightly painted houses and vibrant atmosphere. This small town, often overlooked by tourists, is a feast for the eyes with its cheerful, colorful facades.

Stroll through the old town, and you'll encounter an array of shops, cafes, and historical buildings. The Market Square, with its half-timbered houses and lively ambiance, is the heart of the town. Linz also boasts several museums, including the Carnival Museum, which celebrates the town's festive traditions.

These lesser-known villages and off-the-beaten-path attractions offer a deeper, more intimate look at the Rhine Valley. Each destination provides a unique experience, whether it's the medieval charm of Bacharach, the towering fortifications of Oberwesel, or the colorful streets of Linz am Rhein. By exploring these hidden gems, you'll uncover the true essence of the Rhine, creating memories that will last a lifetime.

Local Lore and Legends

As the Rhine River winds its way through the heart of Europe, it carries with it a rich tapestry of stories and legends, woven over centuries. These tales, whispered through the ages, add a layer of enchantment to your journey. Here are some of the most captivating legends and local lore that you will encounter along the Rhine.

The Lorelei: The Enchanting Siren

One of the most famous legends of the Rhine is the story of the Lorelei, a siren whose beauty and song were said to lure sailors to their doom. Perched atop a steep rock near St. Goarshausen, the Lorelei would sing her haunting melody, causing distracted sailors to crash on the treacherous rocks below. The rock itself, towering 132 meters above the river, still captivates visitors today. As you cruise past, take a moment to listen to the wind; you might just hear the echo of her song.

The Mouse Tower: Bishop Hatto's Punishment

Near the town of Bingen stands the imposing Mouse Tower, steeped in a dark tale of greed and divine retribution. According to legend, Bishop Hatto II of Mainz, known for his cruelty and avarice, was besieged by a plague of mice. In a bid to escape, he retreated to the tower, only to be overrun by the relentless rodents, who devoured him alive. This gruesome story serves as a stark reminder of the consequences of tyranny and greed.

The Legend of the Seven Sisters

High above the Rhine, near the town of Oberwesel, stand the seven rocky pinnacles known as the Seven Sisters. Legend has it that these rocks were once seven beautiful sisters, all of whom rejected their suitors. Angered by their arrogance, their father transformed them into stone. Today, these jagged formations serve as a striking reminder of the tale, their silhouettes etched against the sky, evoking the tragedy of unfulfilled love.

Unique Experiences and Encounters

The Rhine River is not just about majestic castles and bustling cities; it is also about the unique, often hidden experiences that make your journey truly memorable. Here are some of the must-try experiences that will add an extra dimension to your adventure.

Wine Tasting in the Rhine Valley

The Rhine Valley is renowned for its exquisite wines, particularly the Rieslings. Take a detour from the main tourist path and visit one of the many family-owned vineyards dotting the valley. Engage in an intimate wine tasting session, where you can learn about the winemaking process from the vintners themselves. Sip on a glass of crisp, refreshing Riesling as you gaze out over the lush vineyards and rolling hills – an experience that is both educational and indulgent.

Exploring the Timbered Houses of Bacharach

Bacharach, with its beautifully preserved half-timbered houses and medieval charm, offers a glimpse into the past. Stroll through its narrow cobblestone streets, where each house tells a story of times long gone. Visit the Werner Chapel ruins, a poignant reminder of the town's medieval past, and let the serene beauty of the town transport you to another era.

Riverbank Picnics in the Middle Rhine Valley

For a truly tranquil experience, pack a picnic and find a secluded spot along the riverbank in the Middle Rhine Valley. The sight of castles perched on hilltops and the gentle flow of the river provide the perfect backdrop for a relaxing afternoon. Savor local delicacies, such as freshly baked bread, regional cheeses, and cured meats, as you soak in the peaceful ambiance.

Attending a Local Festival

The Rhine region is alive with festivals throughout the year, celebrating everything from wine to music. One of the most spectacular is the Rhine in Flames, a series of summer events featuring breathtaking firework displays and illuminated river cruises. Join the locals in celebrating these festive occasions, where the vibrant atmosphere and communal spirit will leave you with unforgettable memories.

A Guided Night Walk in Heidelberg

Heidelberg, with its historic university and stunning castle, takes on a magical quality at night. Join a guided night walk through the old town, where a knowledgeable guide will share tales of the city's history, legends, and secrets. The illuminated castle, reflected in the river below, creates a breathtaking scene that is not to be missed.

Local Insights and Personal Experiences

While on my own Rhine River cruise, I found that the real magic lay in these hidden gems and unique encounters. One evening, after an exhilarating day of sightseeing, I joined a local guide for a night walk in Heidelberg. As we wandered through the cobblestone streets, the stories of medieval scholars and historic events came alive, making me feel as if I had stepped back in time.

Another highlight was a spontaneous visit to a small vineyard in Rüdesheim. The vintner, a charming elderly man with a twinkle in his eye, shared not just his wine but his life's story, adding a personal touch to the tasting experience that I will never forget.

The Rhine is more than just a river; it is a journey through history, culture, and natural beauty, enriched by the stories and experiences that you gather along the way. Embrace these hidden treasures, and your Rhine River cruise will become an adventure that you will cherish forever.

Chapter 5: Activities and Adventures

Exploring the Rhine through various activities and adventures is a highlight of any cruise. Whether you're a nature lover, history buff, or thrill-seeker, the Rhine offers something for everyone. Let's dive into some of the most engaging activities: scenic hikes and nature trails, and cycling along the Rhine.

Scenic Hikes and Nature Trails

The Rhine Valley is a hiker's paradise, with trails that weave through lush forests, along dramatic cliffs, and past historic landmarks. Each trail offers a unique perspective of the river and its surroundings, allowing you to immerse yourself in the natural beauty and rich history of the region.

1. Rheinsteig Trail

The Rheinsteig is one of the most famous hiking trails in Germany, stretching over 320 kilometers (about 200 miles) from Bonn to Wiesbaden. This trail runs along the right bank of the Rhine and is known for its challenging terrain, stunning vistas, and well-marked paths.

- Highlights: The trail passes through vineyards, dense forests, and picturesque villages. Key highlights include the Lorelei Rock, from which you can enjoy breathtaking views of the river, and the medieval castles such as Marksburg and Rheinstein.

- Difficulty: The Rheinsteig varies in difficulty, with some sections suitable for beginners and others requiring more experience. It's well-signposted, making it easy to follow.

2. Eifelsteig Trail

For those looking for a slightly different experience, the Eifelsteig Trail offers an excellent alternative. Although not directly along the Rhine, it's close enough to be accessible and provides a different landscape to explore.

- Highlights: This trail offers a mix of rolling hills, volcanic craters, and serene lakes. The section near the Rhine, from Blankenheim to Trier, is particularly beautiful, with panoramic views and quiet, contemplative paths.

- Difficulty: The Eifelsteig is generally moderate, with some steep sections. It's suitable for most hikers with a reasonable level of fitness.

3. Boppard Hamm Loop

For a shorter, more relaxed hike, the Boppard Hamm Loop is ideal. This trail offers a scenic loop around the Boppard Hamm, one of the most beautiful bends in the Rhine.

- Highlights: The trail takes you through vineyards, offering spectacular views of the river below. You'll also pass by Roman ruins and charming villages where you can stop for a rest and a glass of local wine.

- Difficulty: This is a relatively easy hike, making it perfect for families or those looking for a leisurely walk.

4. Palatinate Forest-North Vosges Biosphere Reserve

Straddling the border between Germany and France, this biosphere reserve offers a wealth of hiking opportunities. The trails here lead through dense forests, past sandstone cliffs, and to historic sites like the Trifels Castle.

- Highlights: The cross-border nature of this area means you can experience the cultural richness of both Germany and

France. The Dahner Felsenland, with its striking rock formations, is a must-see.

- Difficulty: Trails vary from easy to challenging, catering to all levels of hikers.

Tips for Hikers:

- Wear Comfortable Shoes: Good hiking boots are essential for navigating the varied terrain.

- Stay Hydrated: Carry enough water, especially during warmer months.

- Pack Light: A small backpack with essentials like snacks, a map, and a first-aid kit is all you need.

- Check the Weather: Always check the weather forecast before setting out, as conditions can change quickly.

Cycling Along the Rhine

Cycling along the Rhine offers a different but equally rewarding way to explore the region. The well-maintained cycle paths and the scenic route make it a favorite among both casual cyclists and enthusiasts.

1. Rhine Cycle Route (EuroVelo 15)

The Rhine Cycle Route, part of the EuroVelo network, is a dedicated bike path that follows the Rhine River from its source in Switzerland to its mouth in the Netherlands. This route is over 1,230 kilometers (about 764 miles) long and passes through Switzerland, France, Germany, and the Netherlands.

- Highlights: Key highlights include the picturesque town of Schaffhausen in Switzerland, the wine regions of Alsace in France, and the historic cities of Cologne and Düsseldorf in Germany. In the Netherlands, you'll cycle through charming Dutch countryside and vibrant cities like Rotterdam.

- Difficulty: The route is mostly flat and well-paved, making it accessible for all levels of cyclists. There are some hilly sections, particularly in the Upper Rhine region, but these are manageable.

2. Lorelei Loop

For a shorter cycling adventure, the Lorelei Loop offers a scenic ride through one of the most famous sections of the

Rhine. This route circles around the Lorelei Rock and offers stunning views of the river and surrounding vineyards.

- Highlights: The loop takes you through charming villages such as St. Goar and Oberwesel, where you can stop for a meal or explore local attractions. The Lorelei Rock itself is a major highlight, offering panoramic views of the Rhine Gorge.

- Difficulty: This is a relatively easy route, suitable for casual cyclists and families.

3. Alsace Wine Route

While not strictly along the Rhine, the Alsace Wine Route runs parallel to the river and offers a delightful cycling experience through France's famous wine region.

- Highlights: You'll cycle through picturesque vineyards, past charming villages like Ribeauvillé and Riquewihr, and have plenty of opportunities for wine tasting along the way.

- Difficulty: The route is mostly flat with some gentle hills, making it suitable for most cyclists.

4. Upper Middle Rhine Valley

This section of the Rhine, between Bingen and Koblenz, is a UNESCO World Heritage Site and offers some of the most spectacular scenery along the river.

- Highlights: Cycling through this region, you'll pass by numerous castles, historic towns, and beautiful landscapes. Key stops include Bacharach, Boppard, and the imposing Marksburg Castle.

- Difficulty: The terrain is varied but generally manageable, with well-maintained paths and plenty of places to stop and rest.

Tips for Cyclists:

- Rent a Good Bike: Ensure you have a reliable bike, whether you bring your own or rent one locally.

- Wear a Helmet: Safety first! Always wear a helmet and follow local traffic rules.

- Plan Your Route: Use maps and cycling apps to plan your route and check for any closures or detours.

- Take Breaks: Don't forget to stop and enjoy the scenery. Plan regular breaks, especially in scenic spots.

Whether you prefer hiking through lush forests or cycling along picturesque riversides, the Rhine Valley offers an abundance of outdoor adventures. Each activity provides a unique way to experience the beauty and history of this remarkable region, ensuring that your Rhine River cruise is filled with unforgettable moments.

River Excursions and Boat Tours

One of the most exhilarating ways to experience the Rhine River is through river excursions and boat tours. These tours offer a unique perspective of the scenic beauty, historic landmarks, and vibrant life along the riverbanks. Whether you are a first-time visitor or a seasoned traveler, river excursions can provide memorable experiences that encapsulate the charm and grandeur of the Rhine.

Exploring the Rhine: A Personal Journey

Imagine yourself gliding smoothly along the calm waters of the Rhine, the gentle hum of the boat's engine as your constant companion. The riverbanks are alive with lush greenery, quaint villages, and imposing castles. Every turn of the river reveals a new scene more picturesque than the last. During my own trip, I found myself particularly enchanted by the stretch between Koblenz and Bingen, often referred to as the "Romantic Rhine." This area is famous for its dramatic landscapes and historical sites, making it a highlight for many travelers.

Types of River Excursions

There are several types of river excursions to suit different interests and schedules:

1. Short Day Cruises: Ideal for those with limited time, these cruises last from one to three hours. They usually cover key highlights such as the Lorelei Rock, where legend says a siren lured sailors to their doom, and the medieval castles perched on the cliffs.

2. Full-Day Cruises: These allow for a more comprehensive exploration. You can enjoy meals onboard while cruising past multiple landmarks, often with stops for onshore excursions.

3. Themed Cruises: For a unique experience, consider a themed cruise. Options range from wine tasting cruises to medieval-themed tours where guides dress in period costumes and recount tales from the Rhine's storied past.

4. Private Boat Tours: For a more intimate experience, private boat tours offer personalized itineraries and the opportunity to explore at your own pace. This can be a great option for families or groups.

Top Boat Tour Companies

- KD Rhine Cruises: Known for their extensive route options and excellent service, KD Rhine Cruises offers everything from short sightseeing trips to multi-day journeys.

- Viking River Cruises: For a luxurious experience, Viking River Cruises provides high-end amenities and in-depth excursions. Their boats are equipped with elegant staterooms, fine dining, and knowledgeable guides.

- Scylla AG: Another reputable company, Scylla AG offers both scheduled and customizable tours, ensuring a personalized and flexible adventure.

Highlights to Look Out For

1. Lorelei Rock: This iconic spot is steeped in mythology and provides stunning views. The steep slate rock rises nearly 132 meters above the waterline, and the legend of Lorelei, the siren, adds an air of mystery.

2. Marksburg Castle: The only medieval castle on the Rhine that has never been destroyed. It offers a fascinating glimpse into medieval life with its well-preserved structures and informative tours.

3. Rhine Gorge: A UNESCO World Heritage site, the Rhine Gorge is a breathtaking area with picturesque villages and steep vineyards. It's a must-see for any river cruise.

Tips for a Great Experience

- Timing: Try to schedule your cruise during spring or fall when the weather is pleasant, and the crowds are thinner.

- Dress Comfortably: Wear layers and comfortable shoes, as the weather can change quickly, and you'll want to be comfortable both on the boat and during onshore excursions.

- Bring Binoculars: To better appreciate the distant castles and landscapes.

- Listen to the Guides: Many cruises offer guided tours with rich historical and cultural information that enhances the experience.

Wine Tasting and Vineyard Tours

The Rhine Valley is synonymous with exquisite wine, particularly its world-renowned Rieslings. Wine tasting and vineyard tours are an essential part of the Rhine experience, offering a delightful blend of scenic beauty, local culture, and, of course, delicious wine.

Discovering Rhine's Wine Heritage

The wine culture in the Rhine Valley dates back to Roman times, and today, it boasts some of the best vineyards in the world. During my visit, I was struck by the dedication and passion of the local winemakers, many of whom have been cultivating grapes for generations. The steep, terraced vineyards along the riverbanks are a testament to their hard work and the unique microclimate of the region.

Types of Wine Tours

1. Winery Visits: Most vineyards offer tours that include a walk through the vineyards, a look at the wine-making process, and a tasting session. These tours are a great way to learn about viticulture and sample different varieties of wine.

2. Wine Festivals: Time your visit to coincide with one of the many wine festivals held throughout the year. These festivals are vibrant events featuring wine tastings, local food, music, and sometimes even parades.

3. Wine Tasting Cruises: Combine the pleasure of a river cruise with wine tasting. These themed cruises often feature onboard sommeliers and visits to riverside wineries.

4. Guided Vineyard Hikes: For the more adventurous, guided hikes through the vineyards provide an immersive experience. You can enjoy the breathtaking views while learning about the grape-growing process and sampling wine directly from the source.

Notable Vineyards and Wineries

- Schloss Johannisberg: One of the oldest Riesling estates in the world, Schloss Johannisberg offers comprehensive tours that delve into its rich history and exquisite wines.

- Weingut Robert Weil: Known for its elegant Rieslings, this estate offers insightful tours and tastings in a beautiful setting.

- Weingut Dr. Loosen: Located in the Mosel Valley, a short distance from the Rhine, Dr. Loosen is renowned for its high-quality wines and engaging tours.

Must-Try Wines

1. Riesling: The star of the Rhine, known for its versatility. From dry to sweet, Riesling wines are a reflection of the terroir and the winemaker's skill.

2. Spätburgunder (Pinot Noir): A red wine that's gaining popularity, offering a fruity and slightly spicy flavor.

3. Gewürztraminer: Known for its aromatic and floral characteristics, it pairs wonderfully with spicy food.

Cultural Activities

1. Museums and Art Galleries

- Cologne's Museum Ludwig: Housing one of the largest Picasso collections in Europe, Museum Ludwig in Cologne offers an eclectic mix of modern art. Walking through its halls, you can witness the evolution of modern art from the early 20th century to contemporary pieces.

- Basel's Kunstmuseum: This museum boasts an impressive collection of artworks from the Renaissance to modern times. Each room reveals masterpieces that showcase Europe's rich artistic heritage.

- Rüdesheim's Siegfried's Mechanical Music Cabinet: Step back in time with this unique museum dedicated to mechanical musical instruments. The collection ranges from tiny music boxes to large orchestrions, each with its captivating story.

2. Historic Sites and Walking Tours

- Heidelberg Castle: Perched above the city, the Heidelberg Castle offers stunning views and a glimpse into Germany's medieval past. Take a guided tour to learn about the castle's storied history and its significance in German culture.

- Koblenz's Deutsches Eck: At the confluence of the Rhine and Moselle rivers, the Deutsches Eck (German Corner) is a symbolic site with a rich history. A walk along the promenade offers a mix of beautiful views and historical context.

- Strasbourg's Old Town: The narrow, winding streets of Strasbourg's La Petite France district are perfect for a leisurely stroll. The half-timbered houses and charming canals make you feel as if you've stepped into a fairy tale.

3. Local Workshops and Artisan Shops

- Glassblowing in Wertheim: Wertheim is known for its skilled glassblowers. Visiting a workshop gives you the opportunity to see artisans at work and even try your hand at creating a glass piece.

- Winemaking in the Rhine Valley: Join a workshop in one of the Rhine Valley's many vineyards. Learn about the winemaking process, from grape harvesting to bottling, and enjoy a tasting session of the local wines.

- Traditional Craft Markets: Many towns along the Rhine have markets where local artisans sell handcrafted goods, from pottery to textiles. These markets are perfect for finding unique souvenirs.

Local Festivals

1. Karneval (Carnival) in Cologne

   - Timing: February/March

   - Description: Cologne's Karneval is one of Germany's most famous and lively festivals. The city comes alive with parades, costumes, music, and dance. The highlight is the Rose Monday parade, where elaborately decorated floats and marching bands fill the streets.

   - Personal Experience: Attending Karneval in Cologne feels like being part of a city-wide celebration. The energy is infectious, and the camaraderie among locals and visitors is truly heartwarming.

2. Christmas Markets

   - Timing: Late November to December

   - Description: The Rhine region is home to some of the most enchanting Christmas markets in Europe. From Cologne's Cathedral Market to Strasbourg's Christkindelsmärik, each market offers a festive atmosphere with beautifully decorated stalls selling handmade crafts, festive foods, and mulled wine.

- Highlight: The aroma of roasted chestnuts, the twinkling lights, and the joyful carols create a magical experience that captures the essence of Christmas.

3. Rhein in Flammen (Rhine in Flames)

   - Timing: May to September (varies by location)

   - Description: This spectacular event features firework displays set to music, illuminating the night sky over the Rhine. Different towns along the river host their own Rhein in Flammen events, each with a unique charm.

   - Highlight: Watching the fireworks from the deck of a cruise ship is an unforgettable experience. The reflection of the colorful lights on the water creates a mesmerizing scene.

4. Strasbourg's Strasbourg Mon Amour Festival

   - Timing: February

   - Description: Celebrating love and romance, this festival features concerts, films, exhibitions, and special events in various romantic settings around Strasbourg.

   - Highlight: The festival's unique blend of art and romance makes it a perfect event for couples and romantics at heart.

5. Rüdesheim Wine Festival

- Timing: August

- Description: Set in the heart of the Rhine wine region, this festival celebrates the local wine culture. Visitors can sample a variety of wines, enjoy live music, and participate in wine-themed activities.

- Highlight: Tasting sessions led by local vintners provide a deep dive into the rich winemaking traditions of the Rhine Valley.

Chapter 6: Cuisine and Dining

Introduction to Rhine Valley Cuisine

Welcome to the culinary heart of the Rhine Valley, where every meal tells a story and every dish is a journey through time and culture. The Rhine Valley, known for its picturesque landscapes and historic charm, is also a paradise for food lovers. The cuisine here is a delightful blend of traditional German fare, with influences from neighboring France and Switzerland, creating a unique gastronomic experience.

The Essence of Rhine Valley Cuisine

The culinary traditions of the Rhine Valley are deeply rooted in the region's history and geography. The fertile soil and favorable climate produce an abundance of fresh ingredients, from vineyards producing world-renowned wines to farms offering fresh vegetables, meats, and dairy products. Rhine Valley cuisine is characterized by hearty, comforting dishes that make the most of these local ingredients.

Imagine sitting at a rustic table, overlooking the rolling vineyards, as you savor a plate of Sauerbraten (a pot roast marinated in vinegar and spices), accompanied by a side of red cabbage and potato dumplings. Or perhaps you're indulging in a slice of Zwiebelkuchen (onion tart) with a crisp glass of Riesling. These dishes are not just meals; they are an invitation to explore the soul of the Rhine Valley.

Signature Dishes of the Rhine Valley

1. Sauerbraten: A traditional pot roast that is marinated for days in a mixture of vinegar, water, and a variety of spices before being slow-cooked to tender perfection. It's often served with red cabbage and potato dumplings.

2. Zwiebelkuchen: A savory onion tart made with a yeasted dough, topped with onions, bacon, and a creamy custard mixture. It's especially popular during the autumn wine harvest season.

3. Bratwurst: Sausages are a staple in German cuisine, and the Rhine Valley boasts some of the best. These flavorful sausages are usually grilled and served with mustard and fresh bread.

4. Rheinischer Döbbekooche: Also known as potato cake, this hearty dish is made with grated potatoes, onions, eggs, and bacon, then baked until crispy on the outside and tender on the inside.

5. Flammkuchen: Similar to a thin-crust pizza, this dish is topped with crème fraîche, onions, and bacon, then baked to a crisp. It's perfect for sharing with friends over a glass of local wine.

Top 5 Restaurants for a Rhine River Dining Experience

The Rhine River is renowned not only for its scenic beauty but also for its diverse and vibrant culinary offerings. Here's a selection of the top five dining experiences along the Rhine, each offering something unique and memorable.

1. Hard Rock Cafe Cologne: Set Lunch or Dinner

Immerse yourself in a fusion of culinary delights and rock'n'roll history at the Hard Rock Cafe in Cologne. With a skip-the-line ticket, you can bypass the queues and step straight into this iconic venue. Surrounded by legendary music memorabilia, such as Elvis Presley's sunglasses, Kiss' bass guitars, and Jimi Hendrix's vest, you can enjoy a 2- or 3-course meal. Signature dishes include honey-mustard chicken sandwiches and hickory-smoked BBQ ribs, all served with your choice of drink. Upgrade to a 3-course meal for an enhanced dining experience.

- Duration: 2 hours

- Price: From €27

- Cancellation: Free

- Booking Contact: +49 221 65088442

2. Düsseldorf Brewery Tour (Including 3 Beers)

Explore Düsseldorf's storied beer culture on a guided tour that takes you to three different breweries. Learn about the history and craftsmanship of local brewing as you taste a variety of beers, each with its unique character. This small-group tour offers an intimate experience where you can enjoy a beer at each stop while hearing fascinating tales and facts about Düsseldorf's beer traditions from your guide.

- Duration: 2 hours

- Price: From €27

- Cancellation: Free

3. Sweet Delicacies Tour in Düsseldorf

Indulge your sweet tooth on this delightful tour through Düsseldorf's old town and the luxurious Königsallee area. Visit an array of pastry shops, cafés, and confectioners, sampling delicious treats at each stop. Along the way, your guide will share humorous and intriguing stories about the various sights and locations you pass, making this tour both entertaining and delicious.

- Duration: 2 hours 30 minutes

- Price: From €44

- Cancellation: Free

4. Exclusive Wine & Food Tasting in Mainz Old Town

Delve into Mainz's rich wine heritage with this exclusive tasting experience set in a historic cellar. This small-group tour, conducted in English, offers a curated selection of regional wines paired with delectable local foods. Guided by an expert, you will learn about Mainz's unique wine culture in a relaxed and intimate setting, making it an ideal activity for wine enthusiasts.

- Duration: 2 hours

- Price: From €75

- Cancellation: Free

5. Bean to Bar Chocolate Mini Tasting in Bonn

Discover the art of bean-to-bar chocolate making in Bonn. This mini tasting session introduces you to the process of transforming cocoa beans into exquisite chocolate bars. Sample a variety of chocolates, each with distinct flavors and stories, offering an educational and delicious journey into the world of artisan chocolate.

- Duration: 25 minutes

- Price: Free cancellation

- Booking Contact: +1 786-321-7264

Each of these dining experiences offers a unique opportunity to savor the culinary richness of the Rhine region. Whether you're passionate about music, beer, sweets, wine, or chocolate, these top five restaurants and tours promise an unforgettable taste of the Rhine River's gastronomic delights.

Language and Communication Tips

Traveling through the Rhine region will bring you into contact with multiple languages, primarily German, Dutch, and French. While many locals speak English, especially in tourist areas, it's always appreciated when you make an effort to speak the local language. Here are some tips to help you communicate effectively:

Basic Phrases

Learning a few basic phrases can go a long way in making your travel experience smoother and more enjoyable. Here are some essential phrases in German, Dutch, and French:

German:

- Hello: Hallo

- Please: Bitte

- Thank you: Danke

- Excuse me: Entschuldigung

- Do you speak English?: Sprechen Sie Englisch?

Dutch:

- Hello: Hallo

- Please: Alstublieft

- Thank you: Dank je

- Excuse me: Pardon

- Do you speak English?: Spreekt u Engels?

French:

- Hello: Bonjour

- Please: S'il vous plaît

- Thank you: Merci

- Excuse me: Excusez-moi

- Do you speak English?: Parlez-vous anglais?

Communication Tips

1. Use Translation Apps: Apps like Google Translate can be incredibly helpful. They can translate text, speech, and even images of text. Download the languages you'll need so you can use the app offline.

2. Speak Clearly and Slowly: If you need to communicate in English, speak slowly and clearly. Avoid using slang or idiomatic expressions that might be confusing.

3. Body Language: Don't underestimate the power of body language. Simple gestures, pointing, and miming can help convey your message when words fail.

4. Local Etiquette: Be aware of cultural norms and etiquette. For example, in Germany, it's customary to greet people with a handshake and maintain good eye contact.

Currency and Payments

Understanding the currency and payment methods used along the Rhine River will help you manage your finances efficiently and avoid any unpleasant surprises.

Currency

The currency used varies by country:

- Germany and Austria: Euro (€)

- Netherlands: Euro (€)

- France: Euro (€)

- Switzerland: Swiss Franc (CHF)

Tips for Handling Money

1. Currency Exchange: It's a good idea to exchange some money before you travel. However, you can also find currency exchange offices in major cities and at airports. ATMs are widely available and often offer competitive exchange rates.

2. Credit and Debit Cards: Major credit cards like Visa and Mastercard are widely accepted. However, it's a good idea to carry some cash, especially in smaller towns or for small purchases. Inform your bank of your travel plans to avoid any issues with card usage.

3. Contactless Payments: Many places accept contactless payments through cards or mobile wallets like Apple Pay and Google Pay. This is a convenient and secure way to pay for goods and services.

4. Tipping: Tipping practices vary. In Germany and the Netherlands, rounding up the bill or leaving a small tip (5-10%) is customary.

Conclusion

As you near the end of this guide, I hope you feel inspired and well-prepared for your upcoming Rhine River cruise. The journey along this historic and scenic river is more than just a vacation; it's an immersive experience that weaves together centuries of history, diverse cultures, and breathtaking landscapes. Whether you're a first-time cruiser or a seasoned traveler, the Rhine River promises to offer something unique and memorable.

Reflecting on my own travels along the Rhine, I recall moments of awe and wonder as the boat glided past ancient castles perched on cliffs, each one telling its own story of medieval knights and noble families. The charming villages, with their half-timbered houses and cobblestone streets, felt like stepping into a fairy tale. The warmth and hospitality of the locals, eager to share their traditions and stories, made every stop along the way special.

But beyond the sights and sounds, it's the personal connections and unexpected discoveries that truly enrich the journey. Perhaps you'll find yourself sipping a glass of Riesling in a family-run vineyard, listening to tales of winemaking passed down through generations. Or maybe you'll join a local festival, where music, dance, and laughter bring the community together in joyous celebration. These are the moments that transform a trip into a lasting memory.

Traveling the Rhine is also a journey through time. From the Roman ruins in Cologne to the Gothic splendor of Strasbourg Cathedral, history comes alive at every turn. As you explore these historic sites, take a moment to imagine the countless travelers who have walked these paths before you, each one leaving their mark on this storied river.

Resources for Further Reading

To continue your exploration and deepen your knowledge, I've compiled a list of resources that provide additional insights into the Rhine River and its surrounding regions:

1. "The Rhine: Following Europe's Greatest River from Amsterdam to the Alps" by Ben Coates

   - This book offers a detailed and engaging account of the Rhine River, blending travel narrative with historical insights.

2. "The Lorelei: The Rhine's Famous Siren" by Heinrich Heine

- Delve into the legend of the Lorelei, one of the most famous tales associated with the Rhine, and explore its cultural significance.

3. "DK Eyewitness Travel Guide: Germany"

- A comprehensive guide that covers key destinations along the Rhine, providing practical information and detailed maps.

4. "Wine and War: The French, the Nazis, and the Battle for France's Greatest Treasure" by Don and Petie Kladstrup

- While not exclusively about the Rhine, this book offers fascinating insights into the wine regions of France, including those along the Rhine.

5. "Castles of the Rhine: Recreating the Middle Ages in Modern Germany" by Robert R. Taylor

- A scholarly yet accessible exploration of the castles that dot the Rhine, their history, and their place in modern Germany.

6. Online Resources:

- Rhine Tourism Websites: Official tourism websites for cities and regions along the Rhine provide up-to-date information on events, accommodations, and attractions.

- Travel Blogs and Forums: Personal travel blogs and forums like TripAdvisor offer firsthand experiences and tips from fellow travelers.

7. Local History Books and Guides:

- Look for locally published guides and history books available at tourist information centers and local bookstores along your journey. These often contain unique insights and stories not found in broader travel guides.

In closing, I encourage you to embrace the adventure that awaits you on the Rhine River. Let curiosity guide your steps, and be open to the serendipity of travel. May your journey be filled with discovery, joy, and unforgettable memories.

Bon voyage!

MAP

RHINE RIVER MAP

- Open your smartphone's camera or QR code scanner app
- Point your camera at the QR code to scan it
- Click the notification that appears to open the link
- Start exploring

Made in the USA
Monee, IL
25 September 2024

66598185R00075